Un-f*cking Happiness: A No Bullshit Guide to Emotional Authenticity

Alston Alika Albarado

Published by Alston Alika Albarado, 2024.

UN-F*CKING HAPPINESS: A NO BULLSHIT GUIDE TO EMOTIONAL AUTHENTICITY

First edition. November 12, 2024.

Copyright © 2024 Alston Alika Albarado.

ISBN: 979-8227273161

Written by Alston Alika Albarado.

Table of Contents

"The desire for more positive experience is itself a negative experience. And, paradoxically, the acceptance of one's negative experience is itself a positive experience."

- Mark Manson

*"The Subtle Art of Not Giving a F*ck: A Counterintuitive Approach to Living a Good Life"*

Preface: Welcome to the Shitshow

Congratulations, dear reader! You've just purchased a one-way ticket to the most uncomfortable journey of your life. Buckle up, because we're about to take a wild ride through the treacherous terrain of your own psyche. If you were expecting rainbows, unicorns, and a step-by-step guide to eternal bliss, I've got some bad news for you: you've wandered into the wrong section of the bookstore.

This isn't your grandma's self-help book. It's more like the bastard child of Dante's Inferno and a stand-up comedy routine, with a sprinkle of existential dread for good measure. We're going to dive headfirst into the murky waters of human emotion, armed with nothing but a twisted sense of humor and an unhealthy dose of skepticism.

So, if you're ready to have your perception of happiness turned inside out, your cherished beliefs about positivity stomped on, and your ego gently (or not so gently) bruised, then congratulations! You're in for one hell of a ride. Just remember: I warned you.

Introduction: The Happiness Hangover

Picture this: It's a bright, sunny morning. Birds are chirping, flowers are blooming, and you've just downed your third cup of coffee while scrolling through an Instagram feed full of #blessed individuals living their best lives. You put on your favorite playlist titled "Good Vibes Only" and head out the door, determined to seize the day and crush your goals.

Fast forward to 3 PM, and you're curled up in the fetal position under your desk, wondering why you feel like a steaming pile of garbage despite doing everything the happiness gurus told you to do. Welcome to the happiness hangover, my friend. It's that delightful state where you've chugged the Kool-Aid of positivity and are now experiencing the nasty side effects of toxic optimism.

But fear not! This book is here to hold your hair back while you purge all those saccharine platitudes and unrealistic expectations. We're going to take a sobering look at why our obsession with happiness is making us miserable, and why embracing the full spectrum of human emotion – yes, even the shitty parts – might be the key to actually feeling okay.

Throughout this journey, we'll navigate the treacherous waters of social media comparison, wrestle with the demons of self-doubt, and maybe, just maybe, find a way to be content with our messy, imperfect selves. We'll laugh, we'll cry, we'll question our life choices, and hopefully, by the end, we'll have a more honest and nuanced understanding of what it means to be happy.

So, grab a drink (you'll need it), get comfortable (or uncomfortable, your choice), and prepare to embark on an epic quest through the chaos of your own emotions. It's going to be a bumpy ride, but hey, at least it won't be boring.

Ready to have your world turned upside down? Let's dive in and see just how deep this rabbit hole goes. After all, as a wise man once said, "Abandon all hope, ye who enter here." Or was it "Hakuna Matata"? Either way, we're about to find out.

Chapter 1: The Fall from Grace (Or How I Learned to Stop Worrying and Love the Void)

You're Adam or Eve (choose your own adventure, we don't discriminate here) frolicking in the Garden of Eden. Life is perfect. You're naked, unashamed, and blissfully ignorant. Then suddenly, a snake with a suspiciously smooth sales pitch offers you a bite of knowledge, and boom! You're evicted from paradise faster than a deadbeat tenant on rent day.

Welcome to the human condition, folks. We've all had our own personal "apple moment" when it comes to happiness. Remember that day you realized that life isn't all sunshine and rainbow-crapping unicorns? When you discovered that "happily ever after" is a lie sold to us by Disney and rom-coms? Congratulations, you've just experienced the fall from grace, happiness edition.

The Happiness High

Let's rewind a bit. Think back to when you were riding high on the happiness train. Maybe it was after reading "The Secret" and believing you could manifest a Ferrari by thinking really hard about it. Or perhaps it was when you decided that all you needed to do was "choose happiness" and voila! Instant bliss!

Oh, sweet summer child. How naive we were. We gulped down the positivity Kool-Aid like it was the elixir of life. We plastered our walls with inspirational quotes, meditated our asses off, and smiled so hard our faces hurt. We were high on happiness, and by God, we were going to stay that way forever!

The Crash and Burn

But then, reality decided to crash our party like an uninvited drunk uncle at a wedding. Maybe it was a breakup, a job loss, or just waking up one day and realizing that your life bears an uncanny resemblance to a dumpster fire. Suddenly, all those "good vibes only" mantras started to sound like nails on a chalkboard.

You tried to keep the happiness charade going. You smiled through gritted teeth, posted #blessed on social media while crying into your pillow, and chanted affirmations that felt as hollow as your ex's promises. But deep down, you knew. The jig was up. You had fallen from the grace of toxic positivity, and there was no going back.

The Awakening (It's Not as Zen as It Sounds)

Here's the kicker: This fall? It's not a bug, it's a feature. That gnawing emptiness you feel? It's not a sign that you're broken; it's a sign that you're finally waking up to the complex, messy reality of human existence.

Congratulations! You've just taken your first step into a larger world. A world where happiness isn't a constant state, but a fleeting visitor. A world where sadness, anger, and fear aren't enemies to be vanquished, but old friends dropping by for a chat.

Sure, it's not as pretty as the Garden of Eden. It's more like a dive bar at 2 AM – grimy, a little depressing, but real. And hey, the conversations are way more interesting.

Embracing the Chaos

So, what now? Now that we've been kicked out of the happiness paradise, do we just wallow in misery? Absolutely not! (Well, maybe for a little bit. Wallowing can be therapeutic in small doses.)

Instead, we're going to do something radical. We're going to embrace the chaos. We're going to dive headfirst into the swirling vortex of human emotion and learn to swim in its turbulent waters.

In the chapters that follow, we'll explore this brave new world of emotional honesty. We'll laugh, we'll cry, we'll probably want to throw this book across the room a few times. But by the end, we might just find something better than the illusion of constant happiness.

We might find ourselves.

So, take a deep breath, bid farewell to your innocence, and let's continue this journey through the emotional wilderness. After all, now that we've eaten from the tree of knowledge, there's no going back. Might as well make the most of it, right?

Welcome to the real world, Neo. It's going to be one hell of a ride.

Chapter 2: Wandering in the Wilderness of Emotions (Or How I Learned to Stop Running from My Feelings and Threw a Party for Them Instead)

Congratulations, intrepid explorer! You've survived the fall from happiness grace, and now you find yourself in the vast, untamed wilderness of human emotions. It's a lot like being dropped into the middle of the Amazon rainforest, except instead of jaguars and poison dart frogs, you're surrounded by feelings that want to eat you alive. Fun times, right?

The Emotional Petting Zoo

Let's start by taking a tour of this wild emotional landscape. Over here, we have Anger, a spiky red porcupine that's just itching to shoot its quills at the next person who tells you to "calm down." To your left is Fear, a jittery rabbit on espresso, always ready to bolt at the slightest provocation. And look, there's Sadness, a big blue whale floating in a sea of its own tears.

But wait, where's Happiness? Oh, there it is, that elusive golden butterfly flitting about, never staying in one place for too long. Tricky little bugger, isn't it?

The Great Emotional Escape

Now, if you're like most people, your first instinct upon entering this wilderness was probably to run screaming in the opposite direction. After all, we've been taught that negative emotions are bad, scary, and should be avoided at all costs.

So, what did we do? We built elaborate mazes to escape our feelings. We binge-watched Netflix to avoid Sadness. We drank to numb Fear. We scrolled mindlessly through social media to distract ourselves from Loneliness. Hell, some of us even took up extreme sports just to outrun Boredom. (Because nothing says "I'm avoiding my feelings" quite like jumping out of a perfectly good airplane, right?)

But here's the kicker: The more we ran, the more these emotions chased us. It's like they were playing an eternal game of tag, and we were always "it."

The Emotional Hunger Games

So, what's the alternative? Well, buckle up, buttercup, because we're about to do something radical. We're going to stop running. We're going to turn around, look these emotions in the eye, and say, "Hey there, you persistent little bastards. Pull up a chair. Let's chat."

That's right. We're going to embrace the full spectrum of human emotions. All of them. Even the ones that make us want to crawl under a rock and never come out.

Why? Because emotions, even the "negative" ones, are not our enemies. They're more like really intense, slightly unstable friends who always tell you the truth, even when you don't want to hear it. Sure, they might show up uninvited and overstay their welcome, but they always bring important messages.

The Emotional Potluck

Think of it this way: Life is like a potluck dinner, and emotions are the dishes. Happiness might be the sweet dessert everyone's fighting over, but Sadness is the hearty stew that keeps you going. Anger? That's the spicy salsa that adds kick to your life. And Fear? Well, that's the slightly dubious casserole that might give you food poisoning, but it also might save your life by keeping you from eating something truly dangerous.

The point is, a balanced emotional diet includes all these flavors. Trying to subsist on happiness alone is like trying to live on nothing but cotton candy. Sure, it's sweet, but eventually, you're going to crash, and your teeth will probably fall out.

Embracing the Chaos

So, here's your mission, should you choose to accept it: Stop trying to curate your emotions like they're your Instagram feed. Instead, welcome them all to the party. Let Sadness have the aux cord sometimes. Let Fear pick the movie once in a while. Hell, even let Existential Dread DJ for a night (warning: it's mostly just whale sounds and Radiohead).

By embracing the full spectrum of your emotions, you're not just surviving in this wilderness – you're thriving in it. You're turning it from a scary, unknown forest into your own personal emotional theme park. Sure, some rides might be scarier than others, but isn't that what makes it exciting?

Remember, in this wilderness of emotions, you're not just a lost wanderer. You're the intrepid explorer, the wilderness guide, and the wildlife photographer all rolled into one. So grab your emotional safari hat, and let's dive deeper into this wild, wonderful, terrifying, and beautiful landscape of human feelings.

Next stop: The Temptation of Quick Fixes, or as I like to call it, "Why Retail Therapy and Ice Cream Aren't Substitutes for Actual Therapy (But We'll Try Them Anyway)."

Chapter 3: The Temptation of Quick Fixes (Or How I Tried to Hack Happiness and Ended Up in the Emergency Room of Life)

Welcome back, fellow happiness hunters! If you've made it this far, you've probably realized that finding joy isn't as easy as those Instagram influencers make it look. But fear not! In this chapter, we're going to explore the seductive world of quick fixes – those tantalizing shortcuts to happiness that promise to solve all your problems faster than you can say "self-help guru."

The Happiness Hacking Hustle

In our instant gratification society, we've become addicted to the idea of quick fixes. We want six-pack abs in six minutes, a perfect relationship in six days, and enlightenment in six easy payments of $99.99. And the self-help industry is more than happy to oblige.

From miracle diets to manifestation techniques, from positive affirmations to power poses, we've tried it all. We've vision-boarded our way to... well, a wall full of pretty pictures and unfulfilled dreams. We've affirmed our greatness in the mirror so many times that our reflection is starting to roll its eyes at us.

The Guru Gambit

Ah, the self-help guru. That charismatic figure who promises to have all the answers, packaged neatly in a best-selling book or a weekend seminar. They come in all flavors:

1. The Spiritual Sage: Promising inner peace through the power of crystals and overpriced yoga pants.
2. The Corporate Messiah: Offering the secret to success, which suspiciously looks a lot like working 80-hour weeks and alienating everyone you love.
3. The Wellness Wizard: Convincing you that happiness is just a green smoothie and a coffee enema away.

We flock to these gurus like moths to a flame, wallets open and critical thinking firmly switched off. Because surely, this time it'll work. This time we'll find the magic bullet that solves all our problems.

The Dopamine Dance

Let's talk about the real culprit behind our quick-fix addiction: dopamine. That sneaky little neurotransmitter that makes us feel oh-so-good when we think we're making progress. Every time we buy a self-help book, sign up for a seminar, or start a new diet, we get a little hit of dopamine.

It's like emotional cocaine, giving us a brief high of hope and motivation. But like any drug, the effects wear off, leaving us jonesing for our next fix. And so the cycle continues, our bookshelves groaning under the weight of unread self-help tomes and our bathroom cabinets overflowing with half-used miracle supplements.

The Rock Bottom of Quick Fixes

Eventually, we hit rock bottom. We find ourselves broke, disillusioned, and no happier than when we started. We've tried every quick fix in the book (and several that aren't), and we're still miserable. But hey, at least we can do a headstand and manifest parking spaces like a boss.

This, my friends, is the emergency room of life. It's where we end up when we've ODed on false promises and snake oil. It's not pretty, but it might just be the wake-up call we need.

The Slow and Steady Revolution

Here's the uncomfortable truth: there are no quick fixes. Happiness isn't a destination we can reach by following a 5-step program or popping a pill. It's a journey, and sometimes that journey involves slogging through the mud of our own messy emotions.

Real, lasting change takes time. It's about small, consistent actions rather than grand gestures. It's about facing our demons instead of trying to positive-think them away. It's about embracing the suck and finding meaning in the struggle.

The Beauty of the Long Game

But here's the good news: once we let go of the need for instant results, we open ourselves up to real growth. We start to appreciate the small victories. We learn to find joy in the process rather than fixating on the end goal.

And ironically, when we stop chasing happiness as if it's a limited-time offer, we often find it sneaking up on us in unexpected moments. It's in the quiet satisfaction of a job well done, the comfort of a deep conversation with a friend, the simple pleasure of a good cup of coffee on a rainy day.

The Quick Fix Detox

So, how do we break free from the quick fix addiction? Here are a few suggestions:

1. Embrace the slow burn: Set long-term goals and celebrate small milestones along the way.
2. Practice patience: Rome wasn't built in a day, and neither is a fulfilling life.
3. Get comfortable with discomfort: Growth happens outside your comfort zone.
4. Be your own guru: Trust your intuition and life experiences over someone else's one-size-fits-all solution.
5. Find your tribe: Surround yourself with people who support your journey, not just your destination.

The Final Fix

Remember, the only real "quick fix" is realizing that there are no quick fixes. Happiness isn't a problem to be solved; it's a life to be lived. So put down that self-help book, step away from the vision board, and start embracing the messy, imperfect, gloriously complex journey that is life.

And if you find yourself tempted by the next miracle cure for all your problems, just remember: if it sounds too good to be true, it probably is. Unless it's chocolate. Chocolate is always the answer.

Now, if you'll excuse me, I have a date with a pint of ice cream and my existential dread. We're going to have a long, slow conversation about life, the universe, and everything. And who knows? We might just stumble upon a moment of genuine happiness along the way.

Chapter 4: Battling the Demons of Comparison (Or How I Learned to Stop Scrolling and Love My Messy Life)

Welcome to the gladiatorial arena of the 21st century, where the weapons are smartphones and the battle cry is "Living my best life!" Here, in the colosseum of social media, we fight daily battles against the most formidable opponent of all: everyone else's carefully curated highlight reels.

The Comparison Olympics

Imagine an Olympic sport where the goal is to feel as inadequate as possible in the shortest amount of time. Congratulations! You're already a gold medalist. We've all been there, hunched over our phones at 2 AM, thumb cramping from endless scrolling, wondering why everyone else seems to have their shit together while we're eating cold pizza in our underwear.

It's a special kind of masochism, isn't it? We know it's bad for us, yet we can't stop. It's like watching a train wreck, except the train is your self-esteem, and you're the one driving it off the rails.

The Highlight Reel Hustle

Let's be real: social media is the world's biggest game of "Fake It Till You Make It." It's a 24/7 infomercial where everyone's selling the idea of their perfect life. Your college roommate is posting about her promotion (conveniently leaving out the part where she cries in the supply closet daily). Your ex is flaunting his new relationship (ignoring the fact that they fight like cats in a bag). And don't even get me started on those Instagram "influencers" with their perfect abs and suspiciously smooth skin. (Spoiler alert: it's all filters and Photoshop, folks.)

Meanwhile, you're sitting there feeling like a potato with limbs, wondering why your life looks more like a blooper reel than a blockbuster hit.

The FOMO Phantom

Enter FOMO, the Fear Of Missing Out, that persistent ghost that haunts our every scroll. It whispers in our ear, "Everyone's life is amazing except yours." It's the reason we say yes to events we don't want to attend, buy things we don't need, and post photos of food gone cold just for the 'gram.

FOMO is like that clingy friend who always insists you go out when all you want to do is stay in with your cat and a good book. Except this friend lives in your phone and never sleeps.

The Comparison Hangover

The worst part? After a long night of comparison binging, we wake up with the mother of all emotional hangovers. Our heads pounding with self-doubt, nausea from overthinking, and a general feeling that we've somehow fallen behind in the great race of life.

But here's the kicker: there is no race. Life isn't a competition, despite what your high school guidance counselor might have told you. It's more like a chaotic, multiplayeropen-world game where everyone's fumbling around trying to figure out the controls.

Breaking Free from the Comparison Trap

So, how do we escape this hellscape of constant comparison? Well, we could throw our phones into the sea and become hermits, but let's face it, we'd probably just end up comparing our caves to other, fancier caves.

Instead, let's try something radical: embracing our own messy, imperfect, gloriously flawed lives. What if, instead of curating a perfect online presence, we started celebrating our quirks and failures?

Imagine posting a photo of that cake you tried to bake that ended up looking like a geological disaster. Or sharing the story of how you tripped and fell in front of your crush. These are the moments that make us human, that connect us to others in ways that perfect beach bodies and flawless vacations never will.

The Liberation of Authenticity

Here's the truth bomb: Everyone – yes, even that seemingly perfect Instagram model – is fighting their own battles. We're all just trying to figure out this crazy thing called life, one day at a time.

So the next time you find yourself falling down the comparison rabbit hole, remember this: You are the star of your own unique, weird, wonderful story. It might not always be pretty, it might not always be Insta-worthy, but it's real. And that, my friend, is worth more than all the likes in the world.

Let's raise a toast (preferably with whatever beverage is closest to you right now, even if it's just tap water in a mug that says "World's Okayest Employee") to our messy, authentic selves. Because at the end of the day, it's not about having a perfect life – it's about having a life that's perfectly, imperfectly yours.

Now, if you'll excuse me, I have to go post a selfie of me writing this chapter in my pajamas, complete with the coffee stain on my shirt and the pile of unwashed dishes in the background. #LivingMyBestMessyLife

Chapter 5: The Purgatory of Self-Help (Or How I Tried to Fix Myself and Ended Up More Broken)

———

Welcome to the self-help aisle, the Las Vegas of personal development. It's flashy, it's enticing, and it promises to solve all your problems faster than you can say "vision board." Step right up, ladies and gentlemen, and witness the miraculous transformation of your sad, pathetic self into a glowing beacon of success and inner peace!

The Self-Help Slot Machine

Ah, self-help books. Those colorful tomes of wisdom, each one promising to be the key that unlocks your best life. They're like literary slot machines – you keep pulling the lever (or in this case, turning the pages), hoping that this time, THIS time, you'll hit the jackpot of personal transformation.

You've tried them all, haven't you? "The Secret" had you believing you could manifest a Ferrari by thinking really hard about it. "The Life-Changing Magic of Tidying Up" convinced you that the path to enlightenment was through color-coded sock drawers. And let's not forget that book that told you to talk to your money. (Spoiler alert: No matter how nicely you ask, that $20 bill isn't going to turn into $100.)

The Guru Gambit

But wait, there's more! Why settle for books when you can have living, breathing gurus? For just three easy payments of $999.99, you too can attend a seminar where a charismatic speaker will solve all your problems by making you walk on hot coals. Because nothing says "I've overcome my fears" quite like second-degree burns on your feet.

These modern-day prophets come in all flavors. There's the spiritual guru who promises inner peace through the power of overpriced crystals. The fitness guru who swears you can get abs like theirs if you just buy their $200 workout program (gym membership and plastic surgery not included). And who could forget the business guru who became a millionaire by... teaching others how to become millionaires. It's like a pyramid scheme, but with more motivational quotes.

The Hamster Wheel of Happiness

Here's the thing about the self-help industry: it's designed to keep you coming back for more. It's the Hotel California of personal development – you can check out any time you like, but you can never leave.

You start with one book, but it doesn't quite solve all your problems. So you buy another. And another. Before you know it, your bookshelf looks like the "Before" picture in a hoarding intervention show, and you're still not happy.

But surely, if you just read one more book, attend one more seminar, or buy one more online course, you'll finally unlock the secret to eternal happiness and success. Right? RIGHT?

The Self-Help Hangover

Eventually, you wake up one day surrounded by vision boards, half-filled gratitude journals, and a stack of unread self-help books that's tall enough to be classified as a geological formation. You've tried positive affirmations, mindfulness meditation, and something called "breathwork" that left you lightheaded and questioning your life choices.

And yet, despite all this "self-improvement," you still feel like the same old you. Just poorer and with an inexplicable urge to give TED talks.

Breaking Free from the Self-Help Cycle

So, what's the solution? How do we escape this purgatory of perpetual self-improvement?

Here's a radical thought: What if you're already good enough? What if, instead of trying to transform into some idealized version of yourself, you focused on accepting who you are right now?

Don't get me wrong – personal growth is great. Learning new things and improving ourselves is part of what makes life interesting. But there's a difference between growth and the endless pursuit of some mythical "perfect" self.

Embracing Your Perfectly Imperfect Self

The truth is, you're a messy, complicated, wonderfully flawed human being. And that's okay. In fact, it's more than okay – it's what makes you uniquely you.

So maybe it's time to step off the self-help hamster wheel. Instead of chasing after the next big fix, try sitting with yourself for a while. Get to know the person you are, warts and all. You might be surprised to find that you're actually pretty great, just as you are.

And if you still feel the urge to buy a self-help book? Go ahead. But this time, read it for entertainment, not enlightenment. Trust me, some of those things are funnier than any comedy special on Netflix.

Remember, at the end of the day, the only guru you need is yourself. And if your inner guru tells you to eat ice cream for dinner and binge-watch trashy reality TV, well... sometimes that's exactly the kind of self-help we need.

Now, if you'll excuse me, I have a date with a pint of Rocky Road and the entire season of "90 Day Fiancé." That's my kind of vision board.

Chapter 6: Reclaiming the Garden of Contentment (Or How I Learned to Stop Worrying and Love the Mess)

Welcome to the mythical land of contentment, a place as elusive as Bigfoot riding a unicorn. We've all heard tales of this magical state where people are supposedly at peace with themselves and their lives. But if you're anything like me, you've probably spent more time chasing contentment than actually experiencing it.

The Contentment Mirage

For years, we've been sold the idea that contentment is some sort of final destination. You know, that place where you've finally "made it." Where your abs are perfectly toned, your bank account has more zeros than you can count, and your meditation game is so strong you can levitate.

Spoiler alert: That place doesn't exist. It's like trying to reach the end of a rainbow – the closer you think you're getting, the further away it seems.

The Hedonic Treadmill (Or Why That New iPhone Didn't Make You Happy)

Enter the hedonic treadmill, psychology's fancy term for "why you're never satisfied with what you have." It's that annoying phenomenon where you get something you've always wanted, feel a brief surge of happiness, and then promptly return to your baseline level of contentment (or discontent, as the case may be).

You finally got that promotion? Great! But now you're stressed about the increased responsibilities. Bought your dream house? Awesome! Oh wait, now you're worried about property taxes and whether your neighbors are secretly running a meth lab.

It's like being on a treadmill where the speed keeps increasing. No matter how fast you run, you never actually get anywhere. And let's be honest, most of us aren't exactly marathon runners when it comes to emotional stamina.

The Grass Is Always Greener (Because It's Fertilized with Bull****)

We've all heard the saying, "The grass is always greener on the other side." But here's the truth: The grass is greener where you water it. And by "water," I don't mean "constantly compare your lawn to your neighbor's and then spend a fortune on lawn care products in a desperate attempt to outdo them."

The problem is, we're so busy peering over the fence at someone else's life that we forget to tend to our own garden. We're convinced that if we just had what they have – the job, the partner, the Instagram-worthy vacation – then we'd finally be content.

But here's the kicker: Everyone else is doing the exact same thing. We're all so busy envying each other that we fail to appreciate what we already have.

Embracing the Beautiful Mess

So, how do we reclaim this elusive garden of contentment? Well, first things first: Let's stop trying to create a perfectly manicured English garden and start embracing the wild, overgrown jungle of our actual lives.

Contentment isn't about having everything perfect. It's about finding joy in the imperfections. It's about looking at the weeds in your life and thinking, "You know what? Those dandelions are kind of pretty."

The Art of Grateful Living (Without the Toxic Positivity)

Now, I'm not saying we should all start writing gratitude journals and posting #blessed on social media. (Please, for the love of all that is holy, don't do that.) But there's something to be said for appreciating what you have right now, mess and all.

Try this: Instead of focusing on what's wrong with your life, start noticing what's right. That coffee stain on your shirt? A reminder that you can afford coffee. The pile of dishes in your sink? Evidence that you have food to eat and people to share it with.

Finding Peace in the Present

Here's the real secret to contentment: It's not about reaching some mythical state of perfection. It's about finding moments of peace and joy in the here and now.

It's savoring that first sip of coffee in the morning, even if you're running late. It's laughing at yourself when you trip on the sidewalk instead of dying of embarrassment. It's finding humor in the absurdity of life, rather than being crushed by its weight.

The Contentment Revolution

So, here's your mission, should you choose to accept it: Start a contentment revolution in your own life. Stop chasing the next big thing and start appreciating the small things. Embrace your quirks, celebrate your failures, and find joy in the journey, not just the destination.

Remember, life isn't about creating a perfect garden. It's about dancing in the rain, making mud pies, and occasionally stopping to smell the roses (even if they're actually weeds).

And if all else fails? Well, there's always wine. Because sometimes, contentment comes in a bottle, and that's okay too.

Now, if you'll excuse me, I'm off to admire the "modern art installation" that is my laundry pile. It's not procrastination; it's appreciating the beauty in chaos. At least, that's what I'm telling myself.

Chapter 7: The Alchemy of Meaning (Or How I Turned My Existential Crisis into a Cocktail Party)

Welcome to the existential playground, where we swing between the monkey bars of purpose and dangle from the trapeze of significance. If you've made it this far, congratulations! You've survived the treacherous terrain of toxic positivity, battled the demons of comparison, and escaped the purgatory of self-help. Now it's time to face the final boss: the quest for meaning.

The Meaning Mirage

Ah, the eternal question: "What's the meaning of life?" It's the philosophical equivalent of "What should I have for dinner?" – a question that seems simple on the surface but can lead to hours of indecision and existential dread.

For centuries, humans have been on a wild goose chase for meaning. We've climbed mountains, meditated in caves, and even invented entire religions in our desperate attempt to figure out why we're here. It's like we're all characters in a cosmic game of The Sims, looking up at the sky and shouting, "What's the point of all this?!"

The Purpose Pressure Cooker

In today's world, it's not enough to simply exist. Oh no, we need to have a purpose. Preferably one that's Instagram-worthy and comes with a catchy hashtag. The pressure to find your "true calling" is enough to make anyone want to crawl back into bed and declare sleep as their life's purpose.

But here's the dirty little secret they don't tell you in all those inspirational TED Talks: meaning isn't something you find. It's something you create. It's less like discovering buried treasure and more like making a really complicated cocktail – you throw a bunch of ingredients together and hope it doesn't make you sick.

The Suffering Sideshow

Now, let's talk about everyone's favorite topic: suffering. Because apparently, it's not enough to just find meaning – we need to transform our suffering into purpose. It's like emotional alchemy, except instead of turning lead into gold, we're trying to turn our emotional baggage into a bestselling memoir.

Don't get me wrong, there's value in learning from our hardships. But sometimes, a bad day is just a bad day. Not every moment of suffering needs to be a life-changing epiphany. Sometimes, you stub your toe and the only meaning to be derived is "maybe I should turn on a light next time."

The Connection Connection

Here's a wild idea: What if the meaning of life is... other people? I know, I know, it sounds crazy. Especially if you've met people. But hear me out.

Studies have shown that the happiest people are those with strong social connections. It turns out that while we've been busy searching for meaning in self-help books and silent retreats, it's been hiding in plain sight – in our relationships, our communities, and that weird conversation you had with the cashier at 2 AM.

The Joy of Useless Pursuits

But wait, there's more! What if some of the most meaningful parts of life are the ones that seem utterly pointless? I'm talking about dancing like no one's watching (even though your neighbor definitely is), singing in the shower (much to the dismay of your cat), or spending hours perfecting your sourdough starter (only to forget about it and discover a new life form in your fridge three months later).

These seemingly useless activities might not cure cancer or solve world hunger, but they make life worth living. They're the sprinkles on the sundae of existence – not necessary, but they make the whole thing a lot more fun.

Crafting Your Cosmic Cocktail

So, how do we create meaning in this absurd, chaotic universe? Well, it's time to become the bartender of your own life. Take all your experiences – the good, the bad, and the ugly – and shake them up into a concoction that's uniquely yours.

Add a dash of connection, a splash of purpose, a twist of humor, and garnish with a healthy dose of "who knows?" The result might not be what you expected, but I guarantee it'll be interesting.

The Meaning of Meaninglessness

Here's the ultimate plot twist: Maybe the search for meaning is the meaning. Maybe the point of life is to keep asking "What's the point?" and enjoying the journey of figuring it out.

So, the next time you find yourself in the throes of an existential crisis, don't panic. Instead, invite some friends over, mix up some questionable cocktails, and turn that crisis into a party. Because in the end, the meaning of life might just be to live it – messily, imperfectly, but fully.

And if all else fails, remember: In a universe that's billions of years old, on a planet that's hurtling through space at 67,000 miles per hour, the fact that you exist at all is pretty damn meaningful.

Now, if you'll excuse me, I have a date with my existential dread. We're going bowling.

Chapter 8: Forging Resilience in the Fires of Adversity (Or How I Learned to Stop Whining and Love the Struggle)

Welcome to the emotional equivalent of a CrossFit gym, where we're about to pump some iron... metaphorically speaking. It's time to build those resilience muscles, because life has a funny way of throwing curveballs, and sometimes those curveballs are on fire. And covered in spikes. And possibly radioactive.

The Resilience Myth

Let's start by shattering a popular misconception: resilience isn't about being an unbreakable superhero who bounces back from every setback with a smile and a sassy one-liner. If that's resilience, then I'm about as resilient as a chocolate teapot in a sauna.

Real resilience is messier. It's ugly crying in the shower, stress-eating an entire pizza, and then getting up the next day to face the world again. It's less about never falling down and more about mastering the art of the stumble-and-recover.

The Adversity Gym

Life has a way of enrolling us in its own special brand of boot camp. You didn't sign up for it, you definitely don't want to be there, but here you are, doing emotional burpees while life yells motivational insults at you.

But here's the thing: just like physical exercise, emotional resilience grows stronger with use. Each challenge you face is like adding another weight to the barbell. Sure, it might feel like you're being crushed at first, but eventually, you'll be bench-pressing your problems like a boss.

The Art of Falling Apart (Gracefully)

Contrary to popular belief, being resilient doesn't mean you never fall apart. It means you've gotten really good at putting yourself back together. Think of yourself less as an indestructible fortress and more as a Lego creation – meant to be built, destroyed, and rebuilt in new and interesting ways.

So go ahead, have that meltdown. Ugly cry. Scream into a pillow. Write angsty poetry that would make your teenage self cringe. Just remember to pick up the pieces afterward. Bonus points if you can make a cool new shape out of them.

The Comparison Trap: Resilience Edition

In the age of social media, it's easy to fall into the trap of comparing your resilience to others. You're struggling to get out of bed, while your friend seems to be training for an emotional marathon.

Remember: everyone's adversity is different. Comparing your struggles to someone else's is like comparing apples to existential crises. It just doesn't make sense.

The Phoenix Principle

You've probably heard the saying "what doesn't kill you makes you stronger." I prefer a slightly modified version: "What doesn't kill you makes you weirder and slightly twitchy, but also more interesting at parties."

The point is, adversity changes us. Sometimes it feels like we're being burned to ashes. But remember the phoenix – that mythical bird that rises from its own ashes, probably with a killer new hairstyle and some sassy catchphrases.

Humor: The Secret Weapon

If there's one tool in the resilience toolkit that doesn't get enough credit, it's humor. The ability to laugh in the face of adversity isn't just about being jolly – it's a survival mechanism.

When life gives you lemons, make lemonade. When life gives you a dumpster fire, roast marshmallows. Finding the absurdity in difficult situations doesn't make the problems go away, but it does make them more bearable. Plus, it confuses the hell out of your problems, and that's always fun.

The Resilience Reframe

Here's a mind-bending thought: what if the challenges you face aren't obstacles to your happiness, but the very things that give your life depth and meaning? What if adversity isn't the antagonist in your story, but the wise (if somewhat sadistic) mentor?

I'm not saying you should go out looking for trouble. But when trouble finds you (and it will, because trouble is clingy like that), try to approach it with curiosity. "Well, this sucks, but what can I learn from it?" is a much more empowering question than "Why me?"

The Ongoing Saga

Building resilience isn't a one-and-done deal. It's not like you face one big challenge, overcome it, and then get to coast through life on a cloud of invincibility. Nope, it's more like a never-ending game of emotional whack-a-mole.

But here's the good news: each round makes you stronger, wiser, and hopefully, funnier. You'll develop battle scars and war stories. You'll learn which coping mechanisms work for you (hint: it's probably not the ones they recommend in glossy magazines).

And one day, you'll look back at all you've overcome and think, "Damn, I'm a badass." Just don't let it go to your head – remember, life's always got another curveball ready.

So, strap on your emotional armor (or your comfiest sweatpants – sometimes they're the same thing), and get ready to face whatever life throws at you. Because you're resilient, you're tough, and most importantly, you're too weird to die.

Now, if you'll excuse me, I have a date with my punching bag. I've named it "Life's Challenges," and I'm about to show it who's boss. Wish me luck – I'll probably need it.

37

Chapter 9: The Redemption of Authenticity (Or How I Stopped Pretending and Started Living)

Welcome to the grand finale of our journey through the emotional wilderness. We've laughed, we've cried, we've ugly-cried, and now it's time to face the final boss: our authentic selves. Buckle up, buttercup— wait, I promised not to use that phrase. Let's try again: Brace yourself, you beautiful disaster, because things are about to get real.

The Authenticity Conundrum

Authenticity. It's the buzzword of the century, plastered across self-help books and Instagram captions like some sort of emotional Holy Grail. "Just be yourself," they say, as if it's as easy as putting on a pair of pants. (And let's be honest, some days even that's a struggle.)

But here's the million-dollar question: Who the hell are we, anyway? Are we the person we present on social media? The one our parents think we are? The one our cat sees when it judges us at 3 AM? It's enough to give anyone an identity crisis.

The Masks We Wear

Let's face it: we're all method actors in the grand theater of life. We've got more masks than a Halloween store, and we switch between them faster than a chameleon on a disco floor.

There's the "I've totally got my life together" mask for work, the "I'm a cool, carefree spirit" mask for first dates, and the "I definitely know what I'm doing" mask for, well, everything else. And let's not forget the "I'm fine" mask, which we wear so often it's practically glued to our faces.

But wearing all these masks is exhausting. It's like being in a never-ending costume party where you can't remember which character you're supposed to be playing.

The Great Unmasking

So, what happens when we decide to take off all these masks? When we dare to show the world our true, unfiltered selves?

Well, first, there's panic. Sheer, unadulterated panic. It's like realizing you're naked in public, except instead of your body, it's your soul that's exposed. (Somehow, that feels even more vulnerable.)

But then, something magical happens. You realize that the world doesn't end. Sure, some people might be taken aback by your sudden authenticity. They might even back away slowly, avoiding eye contact. But others? They'll breathe a sigh of relief and think, "Thank god, I'm not the only weirdo around here."

The Authenticity Paradox

Here's the kicker: true authenticity isn't about being a single, unchanging "true self." It's about embracing all the contradictions and complexities that make you, well, you.

You can be a badass career woman who also cries at cat videos. A tough guy who secretly loves knitting. A social butterfly who sometimes needs to hide under the covers for days. Authenticity isn't about fitting into a box; it's about accepting that you're more of a shape-shifting blob.

The Liberation of Self-Acceptance

When you start accepting all parts of yourself – the good, the bad, and the downright bizarre – something incredible happens. You stop wasting energy on pretending, and suddenly you have all this extra bandwidth for actually living.

It's like finally taking off those too-tight shoes you've been wearing all day. Sure, your feet might be a bit smelly, but damn, it feels good to wiggle your toes.

The Ripple Effect

Here's the best part: when you start being authentic, you give others permission to do the same. It's like starting a secret club, except the first rule of Authenticity Club is to talk about Authenticity Club. A lot.

Suddenly, conversations become more interesting. Relationships deepen. You find your tribe – those wonderful weirdos who appreciate you in all your glorious messiness.

The Ongoing Journey

Now, I'd love to tell you that once you embrace your authentic self, you'll live happily ever after in a state of perpetual self-acceptance. But let's be real: that's about as likely as your cat suddenly deciding to respect your personal space.

Authenticity is a practice, not a destination. You'll have days when you rock it, and days when you fall back into old patterns. Days when you bare your soul to the world, and days when you can barely look at yourself in the mirror.

And that's okay. Because guess what? Struggling with authenticity is part of being authentic. Mind-bending, isn't it?

The Final Curtain (Or Is It?)

So, here we are at the end of our journey. We've laughed, we've cried, we've questioned every life choice that led us to this point. But hopefully, we've also learned something valuable: that we're all perfectly imperfect works in progress.

Your authentic self isn't some flawless, Instagram-worthy version of you. It's the real you – messy, complicated, occasionally irrational, but always, always worthy of love and acceptance.

So go forth, you beautiful disaster. Embrace your quirks, celebrate your flaws, and remember: in a world of carefully curated personas, your authentic self is your superpower.

Now, if you'll excuse me, I'm off to have an existential crisis while binge-watching reality TV and eating ice cream straight from the tub. Because that, my friends, is authenticity in action.

And so, our journey ends... or does it? After all, the adventure of being yourself is a never-ending story. Cue the dramatic music, roll the credits, and remember: you're the star of your own show. Make it a good one.

Chapter 10: The New Paradise (Or How I Learned to Love the Chaos and Stopped Worrying About Eden)

Surprise! Just when you thought we were done, like that friend who overstays their welcome at your party, we're back for one last hurrah. Welcome to the epilogue of our journey, where we tie up loose ends, make peace with our demons, and maybe, just maybe, find our own version of paradise.

The Myth of Happily Ever After

Remember how we started this journey? We were unceremoniously booted out of the Garden of Eden, that mythical place of perpetual happiness and bliss. We've spent the entire book trying to find our way back, only to realize that maybe, just maybe, we were chasing the wrong thing all along.

Spoiler alert: There is no happily ever after. There's no perfect state of being where all your problems disappear and you live in eternal sunshine. If that existed, it would probably be incredibly boring. And let's face it, you'd find something to complain about anyway. ("The weather's always perfect? Ugh, so predictable.")

Embracing the Beautiful Mess

So, if we can't go back to Eden, where do we go from here? Well, my chaotic comrades, we create our own paradise. And by paradise, I mean a beautiful, messy, complicated life that we can call our own.

This new paradise isn't a place of perfection. It's a state of mind where we embrace the chaos, dance with our demons, and find joy in the journey. It's where we stop trying to fix ourselves and start celebrating our glorious imperfections.

The Joy of Uncertainty

Here's a radical thought: What if not knowing what the hell we're doing is actually the point? What if life isn't a problem to be solved, but a mystery to be lived?

In this new paradise, we trade certainty for curiosity. We stop demanding answers and start asking better questions. We embrace the "I don't know" and the "Let's find out" with equal enthusiasm.

The Liberation of Lowered Expectations

In our new paradise, we lower our expectations. Not in a sad, defeatist way, but in a liberating, "holy crap, life is actually pretty good" kind of way.

We stop expecting every day to be amazing and start appreciating the ordinary. We find joy in small victories, like successfully adulting for a whole day or remembering to water our plants before they turn into crispy brown reminders of our forgetfulness.

The Community of Misfits

In this new paradise, we surround ourselves with fellow weirdos, oddballs, and beautiful disasters. We create a community where authenticity is the only currency that matters.

We share our struggles, celebrate our victories (no matter how small), and support each other through the rollercoaster of life. Because let's face it, the ride is a lot more fun when you're screaming and laughing with friends.

The Art of Joyful Rebellion

In our new paradise, we rebel against the tyranny of "should." We question the status quo, challenge our own assumptions, and dare to live life on our own terms.

We wear mismatched socks, eat dessert for breakfast, and dance like nobody's watching (even though we know our neighbors are probably recording it for their Instagram stories).

The Practice of Radical Self-Compassion

Perhaps the most important feature of our new paradise is the practice of radical self-compassion. We treat ourselves with the same kindness and understanding we'd offer a good friend.

We forgive ourselves for our mistakes, celebrate our quirks, and give ourselves permission to be works in progress. We replace our inner critic with an inner cheerleader (who's slightly sarcastic but ultimately supportive).

The Ongoing Adventure

Here's the beautiful thing about this new paradise: it's not a destination, it's a journey. It's not something we achieve once and for all, but something we create anew each day.

Some days, we'll nail it. We'll be the zen masters of chaos, surfing the waves of uncertainty with grace and humor. Other days, we'll faceplant spectacularly. And that's okay. Because in this paradise, there's no such thing as failure, only feedback.

The Final (But Not Really) Word

So, my fellow travelers, as we come to the end of this bizarre, beautiful, occasionally profound journey, remember this: You are the architect of your own paradise. You get to define what happiness means to you. You get to write your own rules.

Your paradise might not look like anyone else's, and it certainly won't look perfect. It might be messy, chaotic, and occasionally overwhelming. But it will be authentically, gloriously yours.

So go forth and create your paradise. Embrace the chaos, celebrate the mess, and remember: in the grand cosmic joke of life, the punchline is that there is no punchline. We're all just making it up as we go along.

And honestly? That's paradise enough for me.

Now, if you'll excuse me, I'm off to start a new religion based on the worship of naps and pizza. Who's with me?

And so, our journey truly ends... until the next existential crisis. But hey, at least now we know how to throw it one hell of a welcome party.

Chapter 11: The Cosmic Punchline (Or How I Realized Life is Just One Big Improv Show)

Welcome to the bonus round, the director's cut, the "wait, there's more?" segment of our emotional odyssey. Just when you thought you had it all figured out, life throws you another curveball. But this time, instead of ducking, we're going to catch that ball and use it to juggle our existential crises. Spoiler alert: We'll probably drop a few.

The Ultimate Plot Twist

Remember how we spent the entire book trying to find meaning, build resilience, and create our own paradise? Well, here's the cosmic punchline: There is no ultimate answer. Life isn't a puzzle to be solved; it's an improv show where everyone's making it up as they go along, and the audience is also the cast.

Mind. Blown.

Embracing the Absurd

Once you realize that life is essentially absurd, you have two choices: despair or laughter. And since we've already covered despair in pretty much every previous chapter, let's go with laughter.

Embracing the absurdity of existence is like finally getting the joke the universe has been telling all along. And the joke's on us, but in a good way. It's liberating to realize that none of this really makes sense, so we might as well enjoy the ride.

The "Yes, And" Philosophy

In improv, there's a golden rule: "Yes, and." No matter what ridiculous scenario your partner throws at you, you accept it and build on it. What if we applied this to life?

Life: "Here's a global pandemic!" Us: "Yes, and... I'll learn to bake sourdough while questioning every life choice I've ever made!"

Suddenly, every challenge becomes an opportunity for creativity, growth, and potentially hilarious failure.

The Art of Failing Upwards

Speaking of failure, let's reframe it entirely. In this cosmic improv show, there are no mistakes, only unexpected plot twists. That embarrassing moment? It's now a hilarious anecdote for your next dinner party. That career setback? It's the backstory for your future bestselling memoir.

Remember: The best improvisers are the ones who can turn their stumbles into part of the dance.

The Ensemble Cast of Life

In this grand performance, we're all supporting actors in each other's stories. That stranger who smiled at you? They just gave your day a cameo of kindness. The friend who's always there for you? They're the reliable sidekick in your personal sitcom.

Recognize the roles others play in your life, and relish your roles in theirs. After all, what's an improv show without a little audience participation?

The Joy of Plot Holes

Life is full of inconsistencies, contradictions, and straight-up WTF moments. Instead of trying to make everything fit into a neat narrative, let's celebrate the plot holes.

Why do we park on driveways and drive on parkways? Why is "abbreviation" such a long word? Why do we never see baby pigeons? These are the questions that keep us up at night, and that's okay. Embrace the mysteries. Revel in the riddles. Let your mind be boggled.

The Improvised Self

Remember how we talked about authenticity? Well, here's another layer to peel back: What if there is no fixed, authentic self? What if we're all just improvising our personalities based on our experiences, environments, and that weird dream we had last night?

Instead of trying to "find yourself," try creating yourself. Try on different roles, experiment with new perspectives, and don't be afraid to rewrite your character as you go along.

The Standing Ovation

Here's the beautiful thing about this cosmic improv show: Everyone gets a standing ovation at the end. Regardless of how well you think you performed, you showed up, you played your part, and you contributed to this bizarre, beautiful, collective performance we call life.

So take a bow. You've earned it. Even if you have no idea what you did to deserve it.

The Encore That Never Ends

Just when you think the show is over, you realize it's not. There's always another scene, another act, another unexpected twist. Life keeps going, keep improvising, keep embracing the absurdity.

And if you ever feel lost, just remember the immortal words of the great philosophers Bill and Ted: "Be excellent to each other... and party on, dudes!"

The Final (No, Really This Time) Word

As we close this unexpected chapter, remember: Life is not a problem to be solved, but a reality to be experienced. It's messy, it's chaotic, it doesn't always make sense, and that's what makes it beautiful.

So, step onto the stage of life with confidence, even if you have no idea what you're doing. Embrace the plot twists, laugh at the absurdities, and always be ready to say "Yes, and..."

Now, if you'll excuse me, I'm off to improvise my way through making dinner with the random ingredients in my fridge. Who knows? I might create a culinary masterpiece, or I might order pizza. Either way, it's all part of the show.

And so, our journey ends... until life throws us another curveball. But this time, we'll be ready to catch it, juggle it, or maybe just duck and laugh. Because in this cosmic improv show, the only rule is that there are no rules.

Curtain call, everyone! Or is it just the intermission? Who knows? That's the beauty of it all.

Don't miss out!

Visit the website below and you can sign up to receive emails whenever Alston Alika Albarado publishes a new book. There's no charge and no obligation.

https://books2read.com/r/B-A-KQTSC-OOWHF

BOOKS 2 READ

Connecting independent readers to independent writers.

Also by Alston Alika Albarado

Donors, Dough, and Digital Doppelgangers: An Educator's Guide to Surviving DonorsChoose in the Age of AI
Classroom Wizardry: Unlocking The Magic of A.I. for Teachers
The Grindr Diaries
Un-f*cking Happiness: A No Bullshit Guide to Emotional Authenticity
Paradise Lost and Found: More Misadventures in Chaos

Watch for more at https://books2read.com/alston.

About the Author

Alston Alika Albarado is a Native Hawaiian author and educator who brings a wealth of knowledge and creativity to his multifaceted career with a Bachelor's degree in Drama and a Master's in Theatre for Young Audiences. In his first book, "Paradise Lost: A Journey Through Chaos," he crafts compelling narratives that explore themes of identity, culture, and human connection. His writing offers readers a fresh perspective on diverse voices and local experiences yet integrates universal themes, creating works that are both locally rooted and globally relevant.

Albarado's passion for the performing arts shines through in his background as a musical theatre performer. This theatrical experience enriches his writing, lending a dynamic and expressive quality to his prose and characters. His involvement in theatre also informs his approach to education, bringing elements of performance and storytelling into the classroom. As an innovative educator, Albarado is at the forefront of blending traditional cultural teaching methods with modern technological advancements. He skillfully integrates virtual reality and other cutting-edge technologies into his lessons, creating immersive learning experiences that honor Hawaiian traditions while preparing students for the digital age.

Read more at https://books2read.com/alston.